A Revolution in Real Estate Sales

How to Sell Real Estate

Jim McCord

Revolutionary and Unique Book Publishers

Printed by THE COBB GROUP, Dayton, KY
Printed in the United States of America
First Edition, September 2016
ISBN: 978-0-692-77414-4

A Revolution in Real Estate Sales
How to Sell Real Estate

I've spent the last twenty-three years of my life selling real estate. It's been interesting, to say the least. If only I had had a book similar to this when I began my career in 1993! There were hundreds of books describing how to sell real estate when I received my real estate license. Hundreds more have been written since. I've browsed hundreds and read dozens of them. Each of those books offer some very good information. What I found in almost every book I've read was similar to the advice I was given from almost every broker/manager I've ever worked for. Much, if not all of what they tell you to do does work. However, so much of what they suggest simply is not productive. Most brokers and managers are teaching the same things that they were taught decades ago. They are teaching you to think like a realtor. The information in this book will teach you to think like a seller or a buyer.

Recent books give the same advice but also focus on newer technology. That technology is great and I'm all for it, but be careful. I know numerous agents in my office that are computer gurus. They can do anything with a computer, tablet or phone, but they spend too much time with technology and not enough with real people. Real estate is still a person-to-person business. Using technology is phenomenal and saves us huge amounts of time today, versus twenty years ago. Remember, you still need to deal directly with people to get listings and sell homes.

Most agents leave the industry within three years of becoming licensed. That's a fact. The average realtor in the United States makes less than $35,000/year (National Association of Realtors). If brokers and managers were telling agents to focus on just a few simple concepts, rather than all the ideas they suggest, the majority of agents wouldn't be leaving the industry within three years and the average annual commissions would be much higher.

In this book I'll share unique marketing concepts that have proven more successful than anything I've tried in twenty-three years. It's a simple system that has worked for me and it will work for you. I'll share a marketing system with you which opens doors and builds long lasting relationships that you simply cannot do with any of the other contact managers or any other marketing system, period. It truly is the best system I've ever seen for realtors. There are dozens of good contact management systems and marketing programs available for realtors to use. Some companies have even created their own contact manager. No other contact management system or real estate marketing system can generate listings and referrals as well as the information you'll learn in this book.

What you'll read in this book will be focused on a few simple concepts. There is no magic that will make you successful without hard work. Don't expect it from this book or any other. Utilizing these simple concepts daily, five days a week, is work. Your work will be focused and productive. I've been a licensed realtor since 1993. I've been the top realtor in my county and often the top realtor in my office. Thirty months ago I changed my focus to luxury homes ($1,000,000

+). During my first twenty years in real estate I did not list or sell one home over $1,000,000. In the past thirty months I've listed twenty-five homes over $1,000,000. Now my sole focus is luxury homes. I refer all other business to associates and get referral fees. I can attribute all of those listings directly to this new marketing system. Prior to this system, I was just another agent trying to get a listing. There is no way any of those sellers would have listed with an agent who had not listed or sold one luxury home in the past twenty years! It's an incredible system!

One thing I can promise you, use these few simple concepts daily, five days a week, and you'll have success like never before, regardless which price range you work. I look forward to hearing from any or all of you who actually use the simple concepts presented here.

I do have to mention and highly recommend one real estate book in particular, "The One Thing", by Gary Keller. I was given a copy of this book by a fellow Keller Williams agent the day I joined KW. There is a ton of great advice in this book. The gist of the whole book is to do one productive thing each day and do it before noon. It's a powerful book and great advice for everyone, not just realtors. I have to say it has had a huge impact in my success these past thirty months and is the most useful real estate book I've read to date. If you don't have a copy, get one this week.

Chapter 1

Beware of the Conventional Advice

Why do I say "Beware of the Conventional Advice"? Statistics show that within three years after being licensed, 70-80% of realtors will have left the industry. Brokers and managers have been training realtors pretty much the same way for decades. Sure, they're now including technological changes but the basics are still the same. If what brokers and managers have been telling realtors to do actually worked, the turnover rate would be far, far less. Listed in the next few pages are the strategies most coaches, managers/brokers and books written about real estate marketing are suggesting to realtors.

Door knocking – Going door to door to introduce yourself and build your network. Really? Less than 10% of homeowners will consider moving in a given year. That means you're spending 90% of your door knocking time with people who are NOT even considering a move; not good time management. In a later chapter we'll share how to spend 100% of your time working with people who want to sell or buy a home RIGHT NOW.

Farming – They'll want you to pick a geographical area of homes and mail them on a regular basis. Sounds great! You're building your reputation as the "expert realtor" in their neighborhood. Just as in the door knocking technique, you'll be spending time and money marketing to everyone in that area while only a small percentage are considering a move. Does it really make sense for you to spend money and time working a "farm?" Brokers will tell you to mail to a 500-700 home "farm" on a regular basis. They'll tell you to knock on those doors, make phone calls to the people who live in your "farm" and some even say to deliver pumpkins to those homes. Less than 10% of the population is considering a move during any given year. Do the math. If you're "farming" a neighborhood, you'll be spending 90% of your "farming" time and money working with people who are NOT even considering a move. Really?

Doesn't it make sense to spend 100% of your time and money working with people who definitely want to sell RIGHT NOW? We'll share specifics in the next few chapters.

Sphere of Influence Contacts – They'll ask you to create a list of everyone you have ever known. Input all these contacts into your database and then call them on a regular basis to remind them that you're a realtor and please refer you to anyone they know who may be moving. Before you were in real estate did you want realtors you know calling you three or four times a year to remind you they were in real estate and ask for referrals? Sounds desperate to me. I have to say, yes, it's a good thing to let your sphere know that you are a realtor, but you don't want to shove it down their throats. We'll share later how to let them know in a way they'll actually be glad you're staying in touch with them.

Phone Duty – They'll tell you to take the office phone calls for anywhere from 2-8 hours per week. No! Take no phone duty even if you're just beginning your career. Or if you feel you must, please take phone duty only for a few weeks. Agents do get leads while on phone duty, that's for sure, but your time can and should be spent in far more productive ways. Imagine spending those 2-8 hours per week that you sat on phone duty prospecting directly to sellers who want to sell right now?

Designations and Certifications – Your broker will suggest you take as many courses as possible to get designations and certifications. Well, of course you need your continuing education hours and you need to stay up on the industry but certifications and designations do NOT bring you business. You spend valuable time and money getting those designations that could have been spent getting listings.

Telethons – They think it's a great idea to cold call people (verifying first the prospect is not on the Do Not Call list) over the phone. Do you like getting unwanted phone calls? Enough said. Later, we'll share how you'll never make a "cold call" again.

Weekly Office Meetings and Touring New Listings – It might be a good idea to attend the first few office meetings, and then maybe once a month, but no more. Certainly don't be touring listings. Your time needs to be spent getting business, not meeting with fellow agents, driving to other agents' listings and dining out with realtors. I remember meeting with a developer/builder and a client at a vacant lot I had listed in my second year of selling. About twelve cars pulled up to a home with a FOR SALE sign in the yard. Twenty or so people got out of the cars and paraded into the home. The developer asked me if I knew what was going on at that home. I did because it was a new listing by an agent in my office. I let them know it was "tour day" at the office and all these agents were driving around looking at the newest office listings. Immediately, the developer/builder said "That's exactly why I have you as my listing agent. You're out here with me and a potential buyer trying to get a deal done while those twenty agents drive around". Office meetings and touring listings take at least four hours out of your working week. Imagine spending those four hours/week directly with people who want to buy or sell right now!

Knock on Doors of FSBOs and XPRDs – Not a good idea. At least not until they've received the package you'll learn about in future chapters. You'll see how after they receive a custom package from you, your cold call becomes a warm call and they'll almost always gladly talk to you. Besides, do you want strange people knocking at your door?

Do Open Houses – Yes, occasionally you will sell a home by holding an open house. If your listing is unique, on a very busy street or if the listing is priced aggressively, an open house can work. Otherwise, you're wasting your time.

Computer Classes – Brokers and managers suggest all kinds of computer classes. And yes, these are important. You have to stay up with current technology. However, as stated earlier, don't get caught up and spend more time with technology than you do with people. We're in a people business and it is personal contact that will get you listings and sales.

Chapter 2

Mindset

The single most important concept I can share with you is to change your mindset. Stop thinking like a realtor. Brokers and managers were all trained to think like a realtor. To this day, they still train their agents to think like a realtor. When working with prospects to get listings, think like a seller. Every other agent going after the same listings that you are is thinking like a realtor. You need to put yourself into the mind of the seller. If you were the seller of that particular listing, what would you want to receive? What would you want to hear from a realtor? When you're working with a prospective buyer, think like a buyer. What type of information would you want your realtor to be providing you? What would you want your realtor to be saying at any given time during the sales process?

I've collected a ton of information mailed to and dropped off to FSBOs and XPRDs. I love collecting the information other agents are sending to prospects. It's been a habit of mine my entire career. Simply ask your friends, clients and family to save information that realtors are mailing or dropping off to them. They'll be happy to save it for you. You'll be amazed! All the information is just about the same. It's all about how great the agent and their broker are. Only the company name, logo and agent name is changed. I share some examples of this in later chapters. Be different. Make your information completely different than what all other agents are disseminating. What you'll do after reading this book is personalize your information to that particular client.

You'll stand out because of it. It works and works well!

Sales is 90% building relationships and 10% knowledge. It's hard building a relationship when you're sending the exact same kind of information to clients that every other realtor in your area sends. You need to be different. Your prospects and clients need to know you care about them personally, not just about making the sale!

The "realtor mindset" is to have a canned listing presentation. Agents create a listing presentation, typically sharing how great their company is, how great they are as an agent and they use this same listing presentation with every seller. That amazes me! Every home isn't the same. Every seller isn't the same. You'll want to build your presentation around that particular home, that particular seller and the current market conditions. Do NOT use a canned listing presentation. Almost all the other agents will give a canned listing presentation. Make yours different! It works!

Many trainers and brokers give you exact scripts to learn when talking to sellers and when negotiating contracts with buyers or sellers. I've NEVER believed in memorizing scripts. Reading what some of these trainers suggest is interesting. Some of their ideas are really good. You can use some of their ideas, but I don't suggest you memorize them. I can tell when someone talking to me is regurgitating a memorized script. I'm confident our clients can tell when that's happening also. Talk in conversational tones and don't memorize scripts. Remember, treat people the way you like being treated. You don't like hearing scripts, nor do clients and prospects.

Chapter 3

The Public's Opinion of Realtors

The impression most of the public has of realtors in this country is not positive. They have a negative impression of our profession for a reason. In my opinion, we as realtors have created that negative image. It wouldn't have just happened. At the printing of this book, the most recent Gallup poll shows a 17% high level of trust in realtors. We're right below lawyers and right above union reps. That's nothing to brag about! I decided to become a realtor twenty-three years ago because my wife and I were appalled how realtors treated us while working with us to buy a home. My impression of realtors was very low. I figured if someone got into that field and treated people fairly, they'd do well. Twenty-three years later, after working as a realtor with hundreds of other realtors, my opinion is lower now than it was in 1993. There are plenty of honest, hardworking and decent realtors. However, the chart you'll see at the end of this chapter does put the real estate industry right about where it belongs. All of us have an incredible opportunity because of this lack of confidence the public has in us. Use it to your advantage. Be different. Be the realtor you'd want to have if you were hiring a realtor.

I'm convinced that realtors doing the exact same things that their managers have told them to do, over and over, for the last three decades, contributes greatly to that negative image. Certainly, there are a variety of factors that come into play.

Most realtors list a home and pretty much forget about regular contact with the seller immediately afterwards. The only time the seller hears from that listing agent or that company is when a showing is scheduled or when the listing agent is asking for a price reduction. My focus has always been prospecting expired listings. I hear the same thing from the seller of almost every expired listing - they never hear from their agent. This is amazing to me. An agent needs to have regular contact with every seller.

I can't tell you how many times new buyers have told me that they called two or three other realtors to show them a home they saw in an advertisement, left a message, and NEVER heard back. It happens often. Many realtors do not work full time. They return calls if they want, when they want. Buyers want to buy a home. We make money when they buy a home. When you get a call, return that call the same day. I change the recording on my cell phone every day. It's the first thing I do. "Hi, this is Jim McCord. Thanks for calling. It's Friday the 12th. Sorry I missed your call. Leave your name and number and I'll call you back shortly. Thanks again for calling. Have a great Friday." Then I actually return calls. It's common courtesy. It's how we should treat anyone calling us for any reason.

You can use the public's bad impression of realtors to your advantage. Be uniquely different! Don't talk, act, market or behave like the typical realtor. I let prospects know immediately that I'm different. I am different. I share with them how and why I'm different. I'm always honest with them up front about exactly what I believe their home is worth, what I will and will not do for them and I never make unrealistic promises. I stay in touch with my sellers and give my true opinion to them at all times. Sixteen years ago, at a realtor marketing seminar, the speaker suggested we write these words into every listing contract...

"Seller has the right to an unconditional release from this listing at any time, for any reason."

As soon as he said it, you could hear the agents in the room gasp. They thought it was a horrible idea. I "got it" immediately and have added those words to every listing I've had since that date. It's a way for the seller to realize that if he/she isn't comfortable with me, they're not stuck with me. They have an out of the listing contract at any time. It also keeps me on my toes. I realize I do have to stay in touch with my sellers and do what I said I'll do, or they have the right to a release. It's simple. It's good business and it works. A side benefit of using this statement in all your listings is that if you happen to switch companies, you can take your listings with you. Without that clause in your listing contract, most companies keep the listings when an agent leaves their company.

This Gallup Poll shows exactly what the public thinks of realtors...

	Very high/ High
	%
Nurses	84
Druggists/Pharmacists	70
High school teachers	65
Medical doctors	64
Clergy	56
Policemen	56
Funeral directors	47
Accountants	38
Journalists	25
Bankers	23
Building contractors	22
Lawyers	18
Real estate agents	17
Labor union leaders	16
Business executives	12
Congressmen	12
Stockbrokers	12
Advertising practitioners	10
Car salesmen	7
Telemarketers	5
Lobbyists	5

http://www.gallup.com/poll/112264/nurses-shine-while-bankers-slump-ethics-ratings.aspx

Chapter 4

Three Areas of Focus to Sell Real Estate

Most realtors spend their entire careers chasing the next deal. I did exactly that the first few years of my career. We work hard to get a good listing or a good buyer, work hard to get to the closing table, cash the check and then we forget about them. Of course, most realtors give some kind of thank you gift at closing, and maybe a thank you email or thank you letter, but that's about it. On to the next deal. Statistics show the cost of acquiring a new client is five to seven times higher than the cost of getting referrals from previous clients. Ask most homeowners who they bought a home from five or ten years after they bought the home, and most cannot remember. We're in the business of building relationships, not chasing the next deal.

There are many suggested ways to sell real estate. In my opinion, most books and brokers/managers are sharing far too many ways. Some realtors prospect the old fashion way, door to door. Some prospect via computer. Some prospect on the phone and many don't prospect at all. There are many necessary functions as a licensed realtor that you need to keep up with. Continuing education is one, but don't go overboard on continuing education. Time spent in classrooms does not directly bring you to a closing table. Designations are nice, but they don't directly bring you business and they take a lot of time to acquire. Get designations if it will give you more confidence, but you certainly don't need them to list or sell property. You'll be working with buyers on a regular basis.

You really need to be careful which buyers you're spending your valuable time with. There is maintenance work that needs to be done regularly with your listings. You'll probably want your own website. If you have your own website, make it unique, not the typical site like all other agents and update your site regularly. There will always be agents in the office to talk to. Nothing wrong with that, but it amazes me how many agents hang around a real estate office, drink coffee, talk, browse the MLS and get nothing done in an entire day.

Realtors find so many ways to waste time. Time management is the single most important factor for all realtors. All of us have the same number of hours in a week. The question is, where should you be spending your time?

Here are the three things I suggest you focus on to succeed in real estate. **FSBOs** (for sale by owners), **XPRDS** (expired listings) and **REFERRALS** (building relationships). Focusing on these three areas will make you the most money with the least amount of effort.

You'll get exactly what you focus on. This is true in real estate sales, in your relationships, with your health and with your finances. If you don't focus, like I didn't focus the first few years of my real estate career, you'll get whatever comes to you. I'll share specifically how to successfully focus on those three specific areas in the following chapters.

Chapter 5

For Sale by Owners

Well over 75% of FSBOs (For Sale by Owners) will eventually list their property with a realtor. Why is that? Almost every seller feels their property is worth more than it is. Amazingly, this is almost unanimous. In all my years of listing homes I've had three sellers who actually wanted to list their homes lower than what I've suggested. Almost every seller who attempts to sell without the help of a realtor overprices their home. Overpriced homes don't sell. This is all positive news for realtors. After months of frustration and their home still hasn't sold, they often list with a realtor. Imagine how different things would be if all FSBOs priced their homes correctly?

Most realtors don't prospect FSBOs. It is work, and not easy work. Prospecting FSBOs assures you'll get rejection. Realtors don't like rejection. Those realtors who do prospect FSBOs do pretty much the same things. Many simply go to the door and leave their business card sticking in the slot between the door and the frame. Some of those realtors knock on the door, some don't. Others leave a folder with preprinted info detailing how great they and their company are, along with their business card. Fewer than 20% will actually make follow up phone calls or visits. Sellers rarely make a decision after one contact from a realtor. Selling your services as a realtor is no different than any other sales person selling their product or service. The magic is in the follow up. Most realtors won't do the follow up.

Almost ALL realtors either mail, drop off at the home or both, with the same type of information. It's always about how great the realtor is, how great their company is, or both. Some give a long list of their awards. Some list their designations. Some list homes they've sold or homes they currently have listed. Some list the fact that their company is #1 in that area for selling homes. Some list all of the above, but it's all the same stuff! It's all about the agent and/or the agent's company. Homeowners get tired of seeing the same type of information from all the realtors. The photo below shows actual marketing pieces either mailed to or dropped off to FSBOs and XPRDs by other realtors. Notice all the information is about the agent or their company.

<u>Typical Flow Chart for "For Sale by Owners"</u>

Homeowner decides to sell home on their own... 90% of the time they ask an unrealistic price!

After a couple weeks or months, seller begins to get nervous and is considering listing with a realtor.

Seller begins to save and review information realtors have been mailing or dropping off.

Seller will either meet with someone who was referred to them or to someone who mails or drops the best information.

Almost every realtor in town is mailing or dropping the same type of information with just logo and names changed!

This is where your "Customized card" with brownies or cookies stands out and will get you the appointment!

Always follow up, don't just mail one package and hope to get the listing... The magic in all sales is the follow up! Most agents won't follow up! Follow up and do so with custom cards and gifts!

Using SendOutCards, abbreviated to SOC (I explain this service in detail in later chapters), to prospect for listings is phenomenal. You design your own prospecting pieces. The information they receive from you is now about the prospect, not all about yourself and your company. It turns the follow up cold calls into warm calls. The sellers know who you are and often thank you for the packet you mailed them. It's a great way to establish a relationship! Prior to using SOC, I paid $39 a month to use a contact manager called Top Producer. It was good and it worked for me because I used it daily. However, I was still dropping off and mailing the exact same kind of information that other realtors were dropping and mailing to these same prospects.

Let me share what happened the first time I used SOC to go after an FSBO. It was an $895,000 home on seven acres of land that had been on the market for over a year. A client of mine suggested I go after it. I almost didn't even try because at the time I did not have one other listing in that county, my focus was the county just east of that. One day I was showing homes to a buyer near there and rode by the big 'For Sale by Owner' sign. It was on the second busiest street in the county with a lot of daily traffic. I realized it had been on the market for over a year and I figured even if I got it, it wouldn't sell. However, I knew it would be a great place to have my sign and a great advertisement for me on a busy street. I took three photos, placed one on the front of the card, the other two photos on the inside and added a short paragraph.

Here is that card...

Incredible 7 acre parcel!

Hi Bill,

John Karl suggested I contact you regarding this spectacular property! My specialty is land sales! Hopefully, we can get together soon to discuss getting this parcel sold!

Thanks
Jim McCord

859-866-2354

High Traffic Volume!

Area of Large Estate Homes!

The McCord team specialty is land parcels!

Unique properties require unique marketing!

Four days after sending this card I received a phone call from the seller of the home. He said he received my card, was very impressed and scheduled a time to meet with me the next day. He also told me that he had received over two dozen mailings or drop offs from other realtors over the thirteen months his FSBO sign had been out. He said I was the only realtor he called. Well, long story short, he listed with me. The property sold for $830,000 and I received a $20,000 commission check. I knew then that sending custom cards works. I began sending custom cards like this on a daily basis and discovered quickly that it was more successful than anything I had previously tried.

Here's what I do to prospect FSBOs with SOC.
- Prospect just one new FSBO each day.
- Drive to the home and take a photo.
- Enter the owner and address in the SOC contact manager. (Be sure to check where the tax bill is sent in case the owner lives somewhere else. You want to mail information where the tax bill goes).
- Upload photo of home to the SOC system.

With SOC you can create campaigns which will send multiple custom cards at times you designate to the seller. Send a four card FSBO campaign. They'll get four customized cards from you over the next two weeks. Each card will have the photo of their home on the front. Each card will have reasons they should list with you inside. It's important that the message inside is different on each card. Then follow up with each FSBO you're working on with one phone call a week.

It really is that simple and it works! Those four cards are shown on the next few pages.

Card # 1

This card is sent immediately. I always put the seller's home on the front of the card and include a few short words fitting for that home.

Keep in mind, all the other agents are mailing or dropping off information all about themselves and their company. The seller opens a handwritten, stamped, first class envelope and sees a great photo of their home.

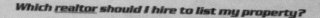

Which <u>realtor</u> should I hire to list my property?

"My friend (or family member) sells real estate."
Use tough standards when selecting an agent, just as you would when hiring an attorney, a doctor, or an accountant.

"The agent who agrees with my selling price."
Some agents tell you what you want to hear. In the real estate profession, this is known as "buying a listing". Pricing your home too high will only make similar houses for sale look that much better and yours WON'T sell.

"List with the agent who has the lowest commission."
Negotiating skill is probably the most important skill in a listing agent. Are you willing to put your faith in an agent who can't even negotiate his or her own commission?

Thousands of dollars are made or lost during negotiating the deal!

I have 21 years of full-time experience negotiating real estate deals in Northern Kentucky!

Jim McCord

Keller Williams Advisors
859-866-2354
jmccordrealtor@gmail.com

Inside of Card # 1

*I address what I've come across as
the three most common objections
on the inside of this first card.*

Card # 2

*This is sent four days after card one. Notice,
I have the home's picture on the front but used
a solid backdrop for the card and included the
"Do Something Different" photo.*

First Name & Spouse Name

There are three distinct phases in all home sales

Pre-sale ---- Preparing home for showings and deciding on a price...
Contract Negotiation ---- Where thousands of $ are made or lost...
Settlement ---- Handling paperwork, inspections and closing...

Buyers today are finding their homes over the internet...
Most buyers call a Realtor to help in their search for a home...
To get maximum sales price in today's market...
1. Your home must be priced "right"...
2. Your home needs maximum internet exposure...
3. You need someone who knows how to "negotiate" the deal...

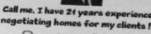

Call me. I have 21 years experience
negotiating homes for my clients !

Jim McCord

859-866-2354

Inside of Card # 2

*More information why they should
consider listing with me.*

Card # 3

Sent four days after Card # 2. I use the same cover as Card # 1 but different wording.

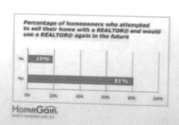

Percentage of homeowners who attempted to sell their home with a REALTOR® and would use a REALTOR® again in the future

HomeGain.

88%

Eighty-eight percent of buyers purchased their home through a real estate agent or broker

AGENTS ARE KEY

The typical FSBO home sold for $184,000 compared to

$230,000 among

agent-assisted home sales.

Fewer and fewer homes are selling "for sale by owner"...

<u>First Name & Spouse Name</u>,
I'd love to see the inside of your home and share exactly what
I'll do to get your home sold.

Jim McCord

jmccord@mccordteam.com
859-866-2354

Inside of Card # 3

Note the above chart I copied from NAR's website showing that 88% of home sales go through realtors.

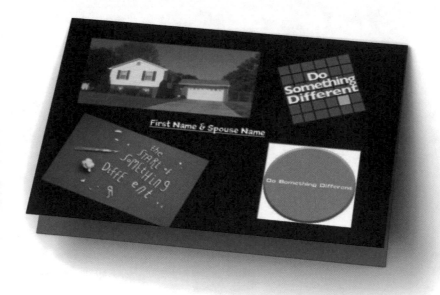

Card # 4

Sent four days after Card # 3. I use a solid black backdrop, photo of the home and the three "Do something different" photos as well. They have impact!

Inside of Card # 4

Often I'll include a box of two brownies with either the first or the last card.

This is what every envelope looks like when delivered. I don't print, stuff, stamp, address or mail the cards. I create them in a few minutes on my computer (or smartphone), hit send and the company prints and mails the cards, all for about one dollar (depending what company plan you've selected).

(Above) When I send the card with two brownies, this is exactly what gets delivered.

(Below) Photo of how other realtors FSBO and XPRD information gets delivered.

Chapter 6

Expired Listings

Without question, working expired listings is the best way to make money selling real estate. Why? Homeowners of an expired listing definitely want to sell their home. They have already been on the market for quite a while. They are probably starting to realize that their home is NOT worth what they thought it was. They are frustrated and irritated by the real estate world. Depending who their listing agent or agents have been, they're beginning to realize that most agents really don't do much to market a home. They typically hear from their agent when a showing is requested, when the agent wants to suggest a price reduction or when the listing is about to expire. However, there are plenty of good realtors out there and many actually do work. In my experience, most don't. This is a huge advantage for those realtors who actually do work to pick up a listing, get it priced reasonably to sell and who then actually market that listing.

There are two other reasons that expired listings are a phenomenal target. The great majority of realtors don't go after them. That's a fact! Prospecting expired listings is work, plain and simple. Secondly, the realtors that do prospect expired listings, almost without exception, do the same things. They either call the seller, if their phone number is available and not on the "Do Not Call list" or they drop pre-printed information, typically in a company folder, to that house. Some don't have the courage to go to the home. They mail the pre-printed package. Either way, drop off or mail, the information they are getting to the homeowner is all about themselves and their company. This is where you can stand out from the crowd using SOC.

Here's what I do to prospect XPRDs with SOC:

Drive to the expired home, take a photo. Have a unique letter saved in your computer that you can print out that morning. This letter will have the home owner's name at the top of the page with the words "Your listing expired at midnight last night." Include a copy of the expired MLS sheet. Highlight the date it expired. In your letter state they'll be receiving a box from you in the mail in a few days. Insert this letter into a unique mailing envelope. I use white bubble wrap envelopes and brown craft envelopes Write the owner's name on the front of the envelope and directly below that write "Confidential". That's all. Don't write their address on the envelope.

Then, back at the office or your home, enter the owner and address in the SOC contact manager. Upload photos of the home into the SOC system. Send a custom greeting card with box of cookies or brownies.

Follow up three to five days after you've sent the package with either a phone call, knock at the door or drop off another letter. They will remember you because they just received a custom card with brownies or cookies. It turns a cold call into a warm call every time. It works!

I'll share two examples: The very first expired home I listed and sold, and another expired home that I just recently listed.

There was an expired listing in my area that had been listed seven times by seven different realtors in the past five years. It was obviously overpriced! The price did get reduced the last two times it was listed. Just prior to this I had listed and sold my first FSBO using SOC, so I figured I'd try using SOC again to get the listing. I sent this card to the owner.

About four days later, the seller called me. He said he was impressed with the card and that he was very frustrated dealing with the seven other realtors. He just wants to sell his home. He said, "Email me a listing contract. I want to list with you. Leave the listing price blank. We'll discuss that when I call you after getting your email. I realize we need to reduce the price." I emailed him a listing contract and later that day he called me back. We agreed on a reduced listing price. He signed the contract and the property sold. Wow, I was excited. It worked! A few months later it sold!

Dale,

Haven't heard from you for quite a while. We met last summer at your place on Camryn! We can sell this place for you! Call me and we'll grab a breakfast or lunch! Hope things are well with you! C ya soon!

Jim McCord

The next card is exactly how I listed an expired farm using SOC. This farm had been listed three times previously, by three different realtors. I had shown the listing once while it was listed. I love listing and showing farms. I knew from showing the farm that it was owned by an older couple. I sent them the exact card you see here. I sent this with two brownies. The seller called me five days after I had the package sent, scheduled a time to meet with me and listed with me at our first meeting. Sending custom cards works because it is so different from everything every other realtor is mailing or dropping off to the sellers.

Mr & Mrs Barth,

Your home has been on the market numerous times in the past few years. No one markets a home like we do. With 46 acres, a pond, barn, fields, woods and a nice home your home needs to be photographed with a drone for a spectacular video and great still shots. Call me if we can get together soon.

Buyers today are finding their homes over the internet...
Most buyers call a Realtor to help in their search for a home...
To get maximum sales price in today's market...
1. Your home must be priced "right"...
2. Your home needs maximum internet exposure...
3. You need someone who knows how to "negotiate" the deal...

Call me, I have 21 years experience
negotiating homes for my clients !

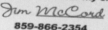

859-866-2354

Here's a phenomenal tip for expired listings! Pull listings that expired one to six months ago that have not relisted or sold. You'll most likely be the ONLY realtor going after these listings. Dozens of realtors will be chasing the listings that expired last night at midnight. Very few, if any, will be aggressively going after listings that expired one to six months ago. Use the same system. Take a photo of the expired home, input the seller's name, address and photo into the SOC website, then send a custom card with brownies or cookies. Follow up three to five days after you send the package.

Chapter 7

Thanking Clients and Building Relationships

Building relationships is what I totally missed out on during my first sixteen years selling real estate. Most realtors don't build relationships. We're all too busy chasing that next deal! That's what we do. We're always looking for that next buyer, or that next listing to get us to the next closing so we can collect another check. We focus so much on the next deal that we forget to build relationships with our past clients. I cannot estimate the number of times that I discovered a previous client, a high school or college graduate or even a friend I hadn't seen in a while listed or purchased a home without using my services. I wasn't angry with them. It was all my fault. I hadn't built relationships with my past clients, friends or classmates. Had I stayed in touch, and in a way that they remembered me and the fact that I am a realtor, I'm certain that most of them would have called me. I'm not exaggerating when I say I'm sure this cost me well over $500,000 in missed commission checks during the first twenty years of my career.

Thank your buyers in a way that they just cannot forget you!

Every buyer who buys a home from me gets a custom thank you card shortly after closing. On the front of the card is a photo of my buyers in front of the home they just purchased. On the inside is a message of thanks with my signature and photo. I usually include a gift card for $50 or $100. Often, especially if my clients have children, I'll include a box of two dozen cookies. The cookies SOC sends truly are the BEST cookies I've ever tasted. I hear this from people I send cookies to all the time. I'll never forget the reaction I got from the first buyer I sent a card to shortly after I joined SOC in 2009. She called me, raved about the card and photo, said she had taken it to work to show her co-workers their new home, then she raved about the Home Depot gift card. She also said the card is sitting on their mantle above the fireplace. Compare that with what I used to do. I'd send a thank you letter on company letterhead to each buyer. Occasionally, I'd give a gift to my buyers at closing. I'm sure buyers appreciated my gesture of thanks, but I rarely heard back from them. I'm sure my thank you letterhead went straight to the garbage after they read it. We all want to get referrals from our clients. Which method of thanks is most likely to get us referrals? Here is a thank you card I sent to a couple who purchased their condo from me. Normally the front of the card is a photo of the clients in front of their home. This couple loved the view from the back of their condo so much that I made that photo the front of the card.

Maggie & David,

**What a spectacular view from your condo!
You two are a pleasure to work with.
Thanks again,**

Jim McCord

I'll share what another very successful agent in my area does to stay in contact with her sphere. She has been using SOC for seven years. Every time she meets a new client, buyer or seller, and before they list or buy, she asks for their birthday and home address. SOC has a system for birthday campaigns where you can set a client up to receive a card every year on or just before their birthday. It's incredible. She takes five minutes to input the client's name, birthday and address into the contact manager. She then clicks the button to send that client the birthday campaign which then automatically sends the client a birthday card ten days prior to their birthday every year. She also includes a five dollar Starbucks gift card. Think about that. Every year, every past client of hers gets a card with a $5 Starbucks gift card. How cool! Do you think she gets more referrals from her past clients than the average realtor? This realtor consistently makes over $1,000,000 a year in commissions!

We're not in the business of selling homes. We're in the business of building relationships. T he sooner you start building and maintaining quality relationships, the sooner your income will skyrocket. T he cost of acquiring new clients is far more, both in time and in money, than getting repeat business and referrals from past clients. You'll read about more examples on how I stay in touch with all of my contacts in later chapters.

Chapter 8

Working with Buyers

Almost everyone who has been a licensed realtor will tell you to work more with sellers than buyers in real estate. It's a fact. Buyers require way more of your time than sellers. You'll be working many evenings and weekends if you work with more buyers than sellers. Get listings, good listings, priced right and then let all the other agents in your MLS work evenings and weekends while you focus on building a good inventory of "saleable" listings. It's easier working with buyers than it is sellers. Buyers actually call you, but sellers you have to go after. You have to work to get good sellers. With buyers, there really is little or no rejection. You show them homes and they reject the homes you show them until they find the right home, but they don't reject you. No matter how long you've been licensed, how many listings you have or how good an agent you are, you experience rejection when prospecting for sellers. It is work but it's work that pays off big time when compared to working with buyers.

That said, you will still be working with buyers. Be selective. Work only with buyers who are motivated to buy soon. Work only with buyers who are "qualified" to buy a home. You might say, well of course those are the only buyers I'll work with. I can tell you, most agents get a call from someone they don't know and spend weeks, months and sometimes years showing them homes without being certain that they are motivated to buy or that they are qualified to buy. Some agents are actually afraid to ask those questions. You'll find that buyers who are motivated and qualified don't mind you asking. They actually appreciate that you've asked. You'll explain to them that when they do find a home they'll be much better off if they can show in writing, with the offer they write, that they have been pre-approved for a loan. It just makes sense.

I have to share a story about a friend of mine who got licensed in 1993, the same year as me. He wasn't good at pre-qualifying buyers early on. He'd work with any buyer who called him to look at homes. One particular buyer had been looking at homes with him for over 6 months. He had shown her over 100 homes. Finally, she shared with him that she had no interest in buying a home. She had a fear of going outside of her home. She thought she'd call a realtor whom she could be with every time she left her home. She looked through the real estate websites, found my friend, who looked like a nice guy, and called him. She thanked him profusely for working with her those past six months and said she was getting over her fears. She also apologized sincerely, but she never bought a house. From that time on, my friend asked lots of questions of every buyer and met them in his office before ever showing them a home.

I like to tip most buyers to other good agents in my office. I'm happy to receive a 30% tip and let them do all the work. I do still work with buyers, but I limit the buyers I'm working with to two or three at a time. Those two or three buyers that I choose to work with will buy soon and are qualified. Today I choose to work only with prospective buyers who I know are qualified and motivated to buy luxury homes.

Always send your buyers a thank you card with their photo in front of home they bought. Include either two dozen cookies, home depot gift card or another gift that fits their needs or personality. They really appreciate it! They'll keep the card and you'll get referrals.

Then, set them up to receive a birthday card every year on their birthday. Include a $5 Starbucks gift card if they like coffee. If they aren't coffee drinkers send a Target or WalMart gift card. This is how you'll get referrals for life!

Chapter 9

Social Media

Everyone has the right to use social media any way they choose as long as what they post follows the guidelines of that media. However, in my opinion, there is a right and a wrong way to use social media for realtors. The right way will get you new business and a lot of referrals. The wrong way will cost you business and further enhance the public's negative opinion of our industry.

Facebook

Facebook can be a very valuable tool for a realtor. Current statistics show that 72% of Americans are now on Facebook*. Use this to your advantage, but don't abuse it. Many realtors post their new listings, open houses and closings on their own Facebook page. Big mistake, at least in my opinion. There are over 1,000,000 realtors in this country. Imagine what Facebook would look like if every realtor posted every listing, open house and closing on their site! Facebook is a social networking site. SOCIAL is the key word here. People go to Facebook to entertain themselves, to learn what their friends and family are doing and to post social things. They aren't going on Facebook to find real estate ads. It's perfectly fine to create your own real estate Facebook page or group and to invite any contacts you'd like to join. This will make your real estate postings available to those who choose to see them and will not be seen by those who are not on Facebook to see real estate ads.

*2015 Pew Research Center statistic. www.pewinternet.org

Here's how I very successfully use Facebook. I "friend" each and every prospect and client I encounter in my real estate career. Some friend me back, some don't. Either way, if they haven't hidden their page, friend or not, I can go to their page and learn quite a lot about that person. It's amazing what you can discover about an individual's hobbies, work, family, etc. on Facebook. All this information is information you would not usually learn until after meeting someone.

Just this year, I got a commitment to list a three million dollar home by friending a prospect on Facebook and sending an SOC package. This was without one phone conversation with that homeowner. I discovered after friending this prospect that we were both long distance bicyclists, both recovering alcoholics and unbelievably, we both were born on the same day. This is really valuable information.

Here's another quick example how Facebook and SOC builds incredible relationships. I saw on a client's Facebook page that he was going to be running his first marathon that next Sunday. Being a marathon runner myself, and now a card sender, I watched his Facebook page that Sunday evening and sure enough, he finished his first marathon. I copied photos of him running the marathon, finishing and his medal from his Facebook page, loaded those photos into my SOC system and then sent him an awesome card congratulating him on his first marathon. Along with the card I sent eight brownies. He couldn't thank me enough six days later when he called me. Think he'll ever throw that card away? I've received three referrals from him since.

People LOVE their pets! When you see that a client or prospect posts a photo of their pet, you have an incredible opportunity. Send them a custom card with their pet's photo on the front. Don't try to sell them your services on the inside of the card. Just send a card with their pet's photo on the cover, that you love seeing photos of their dog or cat and include dog or cat treats to go along with the card from the SOC gifting selection. When they get a package like that from you with photos of their pet with treats and no sales pitch in the card, you have a client for life. It works!

LinkedIn

LinkedIn.com is a business network site. It's completely different than Facebook. Don't post any family photos, cute quotes and certainly don't be posting your listings, open houses and sales here. People all over the country do NOT want to see your new listings, your open houses and they could care less that you just had a big closing.

LinkedIn is phenomenal for finding out what your prospect does for a living, where their office is along with their past business experience. This can be very valuable information. When you can't find a home or cell phone number for a seller, you can often find out where they work. Then get that work number from the web to make your follow up calls. I've been doing it for years with great success. Many prospects have told me that I'm the only realtor who called them at the office. Of course, you'll occasionally get someone who is upset that you called them at the office. That's no different than door knocking or phone calling to homes. It's part of the business of sales. If you're going to prospect, get used to it.

It's equally important that you have a very professional looking page on LinkedIn. Sellers and buyers looking to select a realtor often go to LinkedIn to check out realtors.

Chapter 10

Your Daily Routine

Each morning, get on the MLS and review all homes that expired last night at midnight. Pick one or two expired homes to work. Print those MLS sheets and highlight the date they expired. Have pre-printed letters and unique envelopes in your car. Drive to the expired homes you identified to take a photo. Drop your packet (pre-printed letters and copy of expired MLS listing) either at their door or in their mailbox. Back at the office, input that contact's name and address into your SOI system. Upload the photos you took. Send those expired listings a custom card with a photo of their home on the front of the card and your information on the inside. Include a box of brownies or cookies. Look for FSBO homes along your way. When you find FSBOs that you want to work, take a photo of their home. You don't want to drop anything off at a FSBO. This way, their first contact from you will be a custom card with their home on the front. That's important because when they do speak with you, they'll know you. They ALWAYS remember the card and package you sent. This is what turns a cold call into a warm call. Then back at the office you'll input those prospects into your system and send them cards.

Imagine prospecting just one FSBO or one XPRD listing a day, each day, five days a week. This will take you about one hour a day. Over one year you'll be prospecting two hundred and fifty homes. Imagine how productive this will be! It works!

On a daily basis you should be building your network on

LinkedIn and on Facebook. Connect with at least five new people on LinkedIn and Facebook every day. This will take about five minutes on Facebook and five minutes on LinkedIn. Always connect with your new prospects on Facebook and LinkedIn. It's amazing what you can discover about clients and prospects on these venues. Many prospects you're working to list will be checking your Facebook and LinkedIn pages. Having more mutual contacts with those prospects will add to your credibility. Look for opportunities to connect with them: Their son or daughter graduates from high school or college. They or their spouse got promoted. They went on vacation. They received an award. They opened a new business. These are all opportunities to send custom cards and build your relationships. People love when they get recognized and really appreciate a custom greeting card about THEM.

Make at least one follow up prospecting call each and every day. The magic is always in the follow up. The agent who follows up will always get more listings than the agent who doesn't!

Chapter 11

Dealing with Other Realtors

You'll want to have a good business relationship with the other realtors in your area. Establishing a great reputation among other realtors in your area pays off big time when negotiating offers. Remember, you have a fiduciary responsibility to your clients. Never give confidential information to another agent that could impact the bottom line for your client. I'm amazed at the number of realtors who share things that should never be shared with me while negotiating a deal.

I have to mention one of my biggest issues with some realtors. At the closing table they act like they are running the closing. No, please don't do that. That's the job of the closing agent. Your job as realtor is to sit quietly, answer any questions your client may have about the closing or the settlement statement, thank your client and then gracefully leave with the settlement statement and your check.

Be just as respectful to other agents as you are to your clients. Return calls of every realtor in a timely fashion, just as you do with buyers and sellers who call you. When another agent sells one of your listings, send them a SOC thank you card. Put that agent's photo on the front of the card and include a Starbucks gift card, a gas gift card, brownies or cookies. They'll really appreciate it. Believe me, the next time you negotiate a deal with them, they will remember your thoughtfulness!

Chapter 12

3 Biggest Objections on Listing Appointments

There are many objections that will come up from sellers while you're either in front of them or on the phone with them. The most common three objectives I've experienced are listed here.

<u>One</u>
They think their home is worth more than it is! Often they'll list with the agent who agrees with their sales price. Many realtors will tell a seller their home is worth way more than it is, and the realtor knows this, only to get the listing. That's why in the markets I work in, about half the homes that are listed actually sell. The other half are overpriced. In my opinion, this is the biggest mistake made by realtors. The house won't sell, the seller will get frustrated, and more than likely, will list with a different realtor when the listing expires. Don't list overpriced homes, period. Be honest with the homeowner. Explain to them that listing the home too high will only cost them in the long run. Have the comps with you. Share how long it took the overpriced homes to sell and also share how the homes priced right sold quickly and sold for more than the homes that have been listed multiple times. Let them know many agents will list at whatever price the seller wants but that isn't what you do. Your honesty will be respected and greatly appreciated by most sellers.

<u>Two</u>
Sellers very often list with the agent who will list at the lowest commission rate. Many agents will list a home at almost any commission rate the seller wants. This is a huge mistake.

Here's what I tell those sellers. If that agent can't negotiate a fair commission for themselves, why would you think they will negotiate a good deal for you, when it comes to negotiating incoming offers, to get a fair sales price? Don't negotiate your commission away. Sellers respect this position when it's explained to them.

Three

Sellers list with a relative or friend. This may or may not be a good idea. If their relative or friend is a top agent in the area, I let them know they have a great agent. If not, I explain this is probably the biggest financial transaction in your life to date. Do you want to risk that working with someone who may not be qualified just because you know them or are related to them?

I handle these objections right up front, in a mailing to the prospect in cards sent to them prior to our first meeting. Here's the exact wording I use inside both FSBO and XPRD cards. It works!

Which realtor should I hire to list my property?

"My friend (or family member) sells real estate."
Use tough standards when selecting an agent, just as you would when hiring an attorney, a doctor, or an accountant.

"The agent who agrees with my selling price."
Some agents tell you what you want to hear. In the real estate profession, this is known as "buying a listing". Pricing your home too high will only make similar houses for sale look that much better and yours WON'T sell.

"List with the agent who has the lowest commission."
Negotiating skill is probably the most important skill in a listing agent. Are you willing to put your faith in an agent who can't even negotiate his or her own commission?

Thousands of dollars are made or lost during negotiating the deal!

Chapter 13

The Main Drag, First Photo & Drones

Early on in my career I realized the more name recognition I had as a realtor, the easier it would be to get listings. I have always gone after listings on busy streets with heavy traffic. Most realtors don't go after these listings, thinking it's not likely to sell quickly, so why list it? Getting a listing on a busy street is like getting a free billboard! Thousands of people will see your sign every day. It's a phenomenal place to list homes. There are always plenty of XPRD homes and FSBO homes to go after. Choose the homes on busy streets. You'll get way more exposure this way.

One of the most important aspects of marketing a home is the first photo. This is the only photo that shows on the MLS and on all other websites during an initial search. If this photo isn't appealing, prospective buyers are not likely to click on that listing to learn more. I cannot tell you how many homes I've listed because I showed the seller of an expired home the first photo that their agent used. It amazes me how almost every agent takes a photo of the front of the home, not thinking about the sun, time of day, shadows or if there would be a better photo to use as the first photo rather than the front of the home.

Here's an example of the most recent home I listed using this technique:

(Above) Photo the previous listing agent used as first photo.
(Below) Photo I used as first photo.

This home had been active on the market for over 500 days and had zero showings. We had a showing the second day the home was on the market and the buyer was very interested. The sellers are thrilled with our marketing, especially using this photo as the front photo for their listing!

Drone photography, both still shots and videos are a must with certain properties. There simply is no comparison of a drone photo of a large estate home on multiple acres versus a photo taken from the front yard. Large parcels of land also require the use of drone photography. Once you begin using drone photography and sharing your success with XPRD and FSBO listings, you'll be shocked how many more listings you'll get and how many more showings you'll get from potential buyers. The FAA has guidelines on drone use for realtors. You cannot simply buy a drone and take your own photos and videos. You must use someone FAA approved. Fines are heavy otherwise. Be sure you're using a drone pilot who is FAA approved.

The next two pages show more photos of listings. The top photo is the photo the previous realtor used and the bottom is the aerial photo I used as the first photo. It's phenomenal marketing. I expect aerial photos and videos to become part of all listings, which either are on a large parcel or are considered a luxury home, within the next couple years. Those agents reluctant to pay for drone photos and videos won't be listing much property at that time. As technology changes, it's important to utilize whatever technology is needed to not only stay up with the times, but lead them.

(Above) Photo the previous listing agent used as first photo.
(Below) Photo I used as first photo.

(Above) Photo the previous listing agent used as first photo.
(Below) Photo I used as first photo.

Chapter 14

Focus and Massive Action

In business, in your personal life and in your relationships, you'll get exactly what you focus on. It's important to have focus in a career selling real estate. Make yourself the "expert" in one or two areas of real estate.

Massive action on a regular basis is what makes focus work. You can sit in the office, drink coffee, talk to agents, take eight hours of phone duty a day and read every book ever written on how to sell real estate, but without massive, daily action, you'll still be broke. You're missing out on your true potential. Daily focus, along with massive action, gets results. It's guaranteed!

Most realtors don't have any specific focus. They work any buyer, list any property and try to be the realtor for all who contact them. I did the same for the first few years of my career. Then around year three of my real estate career I decided to focus on single family lots. It worked! I became the king of lot sales in my county. All the developers knew I was the guy to go when selling lots. I quickly became the number one realtor in lot sales. That was great, but there's not a lot of commissions in lot sales. I then focused on selling large parcels of land to developers leading to bigger sales, higher sales prices and bigger commission checks. For the next eight years, I sold more development land to developers than any agent. It was a better focus. Another focus of mine became hunting/weekend getaway land. I love showing large wooded parcels between 50-300 acres. I bought a quad, focused on expired large wooded parcels and became the leader of those sales. As stated earlier, about two years ago I changed my focus to luxury homes. Selling a one million dollar home brings me the same commission as selling ten one hundred thousand dollar homes. Selling a two million dollar home brings me twenty times the commission of a one hundred thousand dollar home. The work is about the same, whether it's a million dollar home or a one hundred thousand dollar home.

Focus on a specific area of real estate. Make it something you enjoy. It could be starter homes, multi-family homes, single family lots, hunting/weekend properties, commercial properties, luxury homes or a narrow geographic area of single family homes. You'll quickly become the expert in whatever area you choose. The public will realize your expertise because you'll publish it, advertise it and your volume will verify it. It works.

Chapter 15

What is SendOutCards?

For the past five years I've used a unique online greeting card and gift system that enables people to act quickly on their promptings. I've found this to be the best marketing tool that I've used in my twenty-threeyears selling real estate. In just a few minutes, you create a custom greeting card, add photos of your choice, write your heartfelt, inspirational or cheerful message and click send. They print, stuff, stamp and mail your personalized greeting cards to any postal address, anywhere in the world, all for far less than greeting cards you'll find in a store. They offer a gifting section where you can choose from dozens of gift cards or hundreds of other gifts, to be sent with your custom card. Buyers love getting a thank you card from me with a photo of them in front of the home they just purchased. On the inside is a note from me and a gift card. You select the amount of the gift card. The cookies and brownies that are available to be sent along with the cards are truly the BEST brownies and cookies I've ever tasted. I hear this all the time from clients I've sent these gifts to. It's truly an unbelievable system. The company is called SendOutCards.

I have to share how I got involved in SOC. A fellow realtor, Brad Cull, had been trying to explain to me for months why I should consider sending custom cards and gifts. I ignored his calls, emails and his invitations to meet because I was not a card sender. I truly had no interest. Then in October 2009, Brad sent a custom card to me. Here is that exact card.

When I received this card I was immediately impressed. I had never received a card with my photo on the front. Instantly, I realized that everyone who bought a home from me should be getting a card just like this but with their photo in front of the home they purchased from me. I called Brad that day and asked him how I could send cards just like this. I'm forever grateful for Brad sharing SendOutCards with me. Without question, it is the best marketing I've done in twenty -three years.

You can learn more by visiting www.sendoutcards.com. Please contact the person who gave or mailed you this book if you'd like more information or if you'd like to join this company. You'll have two options: join as a customer which accounts for over 90% of SOC users, or join as a distributor where you'll be paid when you share this system with others. I suggest you join as a customer, then if you love the product and wish to share it with others, you can always upgrade to a distributor.

Chapter 16

The Power of a Custom Greeting Card

I'm sure most of you have had the "pleasure" of working a short sale transaction. For those who may be reading this and are not realtors, a short sale is when the bank who holds the mortgage on a home has agreed to consider selling the home for less than what is owed on the home. These deals can be incredibly frustrating and can drag on for months and months.

A couple years ago I was representing the seller and a major national bank as listing agent for one of these short sale properties. We had two buyers who wrote offers back out of the deal because the process was taking way too long. Each deal had drug on for months. The buyers became frustrated and walked away. The third set of buyers who had written a contract were very frustrated with this process and they also were about to release and walk away from the deal. I was frustrated. So frustrated that I had decided if these buyers walk from the deal, I'd release the listing and move on. I decided to send the CEO of this national bank a custom greeting card to see if I could get him involved. I created a card with the CEO's photo on the front along with a personal quote of his that I found on the internet. On the inside of this card I described the frustration of the short sale process with his bank, the fact that his bank had already lost over $20,000 because of the incredibly slow way their short sale department handles these transactions and asked him to contact me. I included a gift wrapped box of two dozen cookies. Five days after I sent the package, this CEO contacted me. We talked for about twenty minutes over the phone. This property closed the next Friday for just under $200,000. I made a $5,000 commission check because I sent a custom card with two dozen cookies to the CEO of a Fortune 500 company.

Chapter 17

Sharing SendOutCards With Others

How would you like to be paid from the vendors or companies you have been using to market your real estate services? Wouldn't it be great if the local board that you pay dues to every quarter, Top Producer, or that magazine or publication you advertise in paid you? Can you imagine them paying you? Well, that's what happens if you join SOC as a distributor and share it with other people. I know this sounds too good to be true, but it's not. That's exactly what I've experienced these past five years as a user and distributor in SOC. SOC has paid me, in distributor checks, more than what I've paid SOC to mail all the cards I've sent. On top of that, I can directly attribute over $200,000 of additional real estate commissions I've made in the past five years to SOC. That's $200,000 on top of what I would have made without SOC.

Every realtor should be using this system to prospect for new business, to thank buyers and to build lasting relationships with past clients, schoolmates and everyone they know. Sharing this phenomenal system will accomplish two things. That realtor will appreciate you forever, since you share an incredible marketing system with them. And you'll receive checks from SOC as you build more and more users and distributors under you.

It's an incredible opportunity! When you find a great new

restaurant with awesome food, don't you like to share that with your friends and family? When you've tried a recipe that everyone loves, don't you enjoy sharing it with others? It's fun to share things you enjoy. SOC is a system that realtors are looking for. You might as well be the one who shares it and gets paid!

Chapter 18

Testimonial from Another Realtor Using SOC

Hundreds of realtors around the country are experiencing the same success I am by incorporating SOC into their marketing plan.

"SendOutCards has been the tool for increasing my business year over year since 2008. Moreover, it is cemented relationships in sales for our team along with educating our vendors on how they can increase their own business. Teaching real estate business partners on how SOC helps us all has positively impacted our collective business together.

On the owner side of my business, SendOutCards has truly rocketed our firm as the best place to work here in New England. Growing from 53 agents in 2008 to nearly 320 agents in 2015 while fighting off a recession and parting from our franchise surely demonstrates that we are doing things differently than our competition. I can say without question SendOutCards has and continues to have a significant influence in this success...."

Jay Mchugh, Broker/Owner LAER Realty Partners, Danvers, MA

Chapter 19

Using SendOutCards in Your Personal Life

Other than our four wonderful children, nothing has changed my life in a positive way more than using SOC! Sending out custom greeting cards has not only become a daily habit, but it's made me a better person. It's incredible, really! What's hilarious about this is the fact that prior to 2009, when Brad Cull first shared SOC with me, I hadn't ever mailed a greeting card. Not one card! I never even mailed Christmas cards to my family, friends or real estate clients. I just wasn't a card sender. People love getting greeting cards with photos of them or their children on the card. We live in a world of texts, emails, tweets, Facebook messages and phone calls. Receiving a custom greeting card in the mail has great impact.

In November 2011, I mailed a greeting card to the division manager of White Castle, a local fast food restaurant, and one to the manager of the White Castle restaurant that I frequent. One particular employee who works there is ALWAYS upbeat and positive. She just makes my day every time I stop there to get coffee. I wanted to thank her in a very positive way. I sent a card to her manager and the division manager. On the cover of this card was the photo of that employee. On the inside was a description of how wonderful she is every time I go through the drive-through, how unusual it is to run into a fast food worker with such a positive attitude. I included a $25 gift card and asked the division manager to give to her. About five weeks later when I was getting coffee at the drive-through, the employee shared what happened. She was so grateful and smiling even more than usual as she shared the story. The division manager of White Castle drove down to Kentucky with the CEO and a few others to celebrate what was supposed to be an employee appreciation dinner for all the employees at that location. At the beginning of the dinner, the division manager asked her to come to the front of the room. He said they had driven down to honor her only. He held up the card I had sent, said he received this card from a customer of the restaurant and then he read my card. He gave her my $25 gift card and then gave her another $100 gift card from the company. He then introduced the manager of the restaurant who read the card I had sent to him and two more gift cards were presented to her.

To this day, they treat me very well at this restaurant. Needless to say, she was very pleased.

My favorite card story (and I have a lot of card stories) is a card I created for my son to get an interview. My son is a pilot. He was flying for an airline in the northeast, making starting pay for a pilot, which is very, very low. He really wanted to get a job flying for a local shuttle airline. He shared with me that he had dropped off his resume, made numerous calls to the chief pilot who does the hiring, but never got an interview. He really wanted to work for this company as their pilots are back home almost every night and he would be paid twice what he was making. Where he was working, he was staying in hotels throughout the northeast. We sent a card with the company's logo and jet on the front, with a request for an interview on the inside. We sent this with two dozen cookies in a gift wrapped box. My son was reluctant and didn't think it would work but he let me send the package. About a week later, my son called me. He said, and I'll never forget, "Dad, you're a friggin' genius!" He had never told me that before, so I asked him why he would say that. He said the chief pilot called him, said he had been hiring pilots for fifteen years and never got a package like what my son had sent him. He asked my son to come in for the interview. He got the job! The card and cookies didn't get him the job; he got the job because he's a great pilot, had enough hours, great references and interviewed well. However, it was the card and cookies that got him the interview. It works!

I could relate at least twenty personal stories, somewhat similar to these that have happened since I began sending custom cards through SOC. What's so unusual is that I never, ever sent thank you cards or gifts in my life until I joined. I love being able to celebrate the lives of people I meet in such an awesome and easy fashion. This truly is a life-changing company.

Conclusion

I read somewhere that every realtor should ask themselves this question...

"If you were an employer and had you as an employee, working the way you work on a daily basis, would you keep you as an employee or would you fire yourself?"

I love that question. I can honestly say for many of the years that I sold real estate, I'd fire myself. Having asked dozens of realtors this question, I get the same response from all of the HONEST realtors. Working as a realtor, we're considered a private contractor. We don't have a boss. That's a blessing and a curse. It's a blessing because we really don't have a boss. It's a curse because if we're burned out on work, frustrated or depressed, we don't have to work on any given day. When we were employees, working for a boss at a "real company" we had to show up every day, five days a week, and we had to work. Not the case when you're a realtor. Ask yourself each and every week...

"If you were an employer and had you as an employee, working the way you work on a daily basis, would you keep you as an employee or would you fire yourself?"

As I mentioned in the very beginning of this book, I've read dozens and dozens of books on how to sell real estate. Without question, the book that has made the biggest impact in my real estate career is "The One Thing" by Gary Keller. If you haven't read that, please order it immediately. It's truly the best book written to date to impact your real estate career! Use what you've learned here to stand apart from the realtors in your area. Always have the mindset of a seller or a buyer, not a realtor. Be different than all the other realtors. Be the kind of realtor you'd want to hire. Prospect XPRDs and FSBOs daily with the systems described in this book. Build productive relationships with your past and future clients. Be uniquely different. It works!

About the Author

Jim McCord has been a licensed realtor since 1993. He has worked for local, regional and nationwide real estate firms. Jim is currently licensed with Keller Williams in Cincinnati, OH and lives in Ft. Thomas, KY. He no longer sells real estate as he now coaches realtors nationwide full time. He has four grown children, four grandchildren, loves to travel, hike, bike and run. In 1978 he rode a bicycle from Williamsburg, VA to Florence, OR. In 2002 he ran a marathon a day from San Diego, CA until he reached Washington, DC for diabetes awareness. He has a passion for helping and conversing with homeless people.

ARevolutionInRealEstate.com
SendOutCards.com/jimmccord
Search Jim McCord Realtor on Youtube.com
Search Jim McCord Realtor on Facebook and Linkedin
jmccordrealtor@gmail.com
859-866-2354